mxm

maximalist interiors

mxm
maximalist interiors

Edited by Encarna Castillo

HARPER DESIGN international

An Imprint of HarperCollins*Publishers*

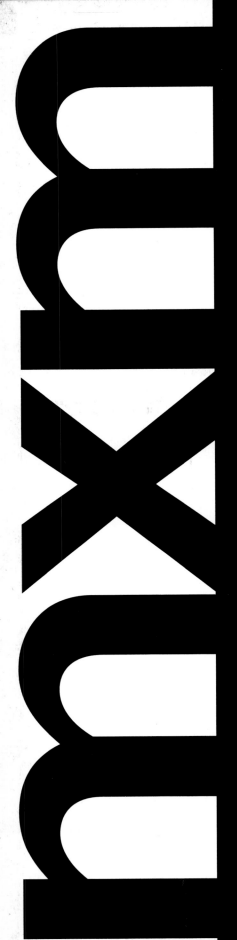

Publisher: **Paco Asensio**

Editor in Chief: **Haike Falkenberg**

Editorial Coordination and Text: **Encarna Castillo**

English Text: **Madeline Carey**

Art Director: **Mireia Casanovas Soley**

Graphic Design & Layout: **Miguel Ángel Ramos López**

First published in 2003 by:
Harper Design International, an imprint of HarperCollins Publishers
10 East 53rd Street
New York, NY 10022

Distributed throughout the world by:
HarperCollins International
10 East 53rd Street
New York, NY 10022
Tel.: (212) 207-7000
Fax: (212) 207-7654

HarperCollins books may be purchased for educational, business, or sales promotional
use. For information, please write:
Special Markets Department
HarperCollins Publishers Inc.
10 East 53rd Street
New York, NY 10022

Library of Congress Control Number: 2003109565

ISBN: 0-06-056757-0
DL: B-28220-03

Editorial project

LOFT Publications
Via Laietana, 32 4º Of. 92
08003 Barcelona. Spain
Tel.: +34 932 688 088
Fax: +34 932 687 073
e-mail: loft@loftpublications.com
www.loftpublications.com

Printed by:
Anman Gràfiques del Vallès, Spain

July 2003

Interior design is the result of the interaction between the personality of whoever lives in a home and pure expression, be it through assimilation and imitation or through complete rejection of the current era. Within this coexistence between personality and expression, it is interesting to observe the cases in which individual creative force overtakes dominating trends and creates expressive personal forms.

As in most turn-of-the-century periods, today many new and old trends coexist and have formed a new and ample mosaic. The last half of the twentieth century, which has affected the present the most, was marked by very defined aesthetic tendencies, such as pop during the sixties, funk during the seventies or high-tech during the eighties and nineties, although these trends obviously all extend beyond the time boundaries set by critics. The twenty-first century has yet to find a clear, radically different aesthetic; the earlier trends continue to coexist, adapting and reinventing themselves, and they have been revisited on numerous occasions.

Maximalism in interior design is the reflection of a society influenced by constant and varied revivals and by the recycling of fashions as well as ideologies. One of the most common is the return to the seventies, marked by an aesthetic which yearns for the excesses in clothing and decorating as a metaphor for a decade that was much more open to the voluptuous and the sensual and sometimes mixed with hippie elements in which color and volumetric shapes monopolize space. Another frequent revival is the return to the eighteenth, nineteenth, and early twentieth century where elegance and sophistication create a "gilded cage" or "marble tower" which rebel against the grayness, uniformity, and boringness of an age that has made a brand name out of unattractiveness and industrial repetition. On the other hand, pop's democratic formulas have put expressive forms into the reach of anyone interested in art and aesthetics, and they have allowed for the use of color and inexpensive materials as well as the de-contextualization of certain elements, such as brand name ads or neon signs used in decorative contexts.

MINI-TREATISE.

MAXIMALism INVOLVES THE INDIVIDUAL
USE OF ORDER TO CREATE CHAOS,
AND VICE-VERSA,
IN THE TRADITION OF THE HIGH/LOW
ART EXPERIENCE OF LIFE-FORCE
THROUGH SELF AND SURROUNDINGS,
BOTH INNER AND OUTER,
BE IT IN GALLERY OR GUTTER,
NECESSARY FOR SURVIVAL AND IT'S GLORY
EXPRESSED THROUGH IMAGES THAT HAUNT
THE IMAGINATION
THROUGH COLOUR/FORM AND CONTENT,
TO GROWTH BOTH PERSONAL AND SOCIETAL,
IN THE ACCEPTANCE AND CELEBRATION OF
THE ON-GOING CHANGE THAT IS
THE ONLY CONSTANCY OF LIFE/DEATH,
WHOSE LOGIC IS WITTY,
SOMETIMES.

Image: Duggie Fields

Excess and exuberance characterize these maximalist interiors. In some cases these excesses are based in the ornamental details; in others they come from the vibrancy of colors and even the magnificence of timeless luxury. Often there is a nostalgia for a past that respected convention and high culture. Some of these trends have already been baptized with a name, like new baroque, which consists of recapturing baroque and rococo elements that coexist alongside contemporary elements. Sometimes this style of decorating is the expression of a personal philosophy, a way of understanding the world, or an artistic investigation of light and color. We also see the option of adapting chromatic ranges and shapes offered by nature itself, with ethnic elements chosen personally or, in other cases, due to economic limitations—as is the case in more modest constructions where natural resources are used as inexpensive ornamental materials—The other fundamental resource of this decorating style is recycling; in most of these projects there are elements that have been used before, and this de-contextualization empowers the art and beauty. And, on the other hand, recycling lowers the cost because these elements with lots of personality can be found in secondhand shops or flea markets, and are sometimes even found on the street or other places where they are not being used. However, at other times it is quite the contrary and these pieces are antiques. Maximalism is a personal rebellion against the uniformity and standardization of the formulas proposed by minimalism—which has been elevated to a canon of beauty—and a demand for other ways of understanding space and the individual's relationship to it.

MAXIMAL ARTefact.

MINIMALism, LESS IS LESS, MORE OR LESS,
LEADS TO STASIS. IT IS OVERCOME BY GRAVITY.
OVERDUE FOR THE INEVITABLE CHANGE.
MAXIMALism, IT'S BIGGER LITTLE BROTHER,
IS THE NEW CAUSE CELEBRE.

INCLUDE ALL EXCLUSIVELY.
CONQUER DIVISIVE IDEOLOGY.
MAXIMISE TO THE MAX.

SOMETIMES.

Image: Duggie Fields

Trois

Hassan Abdullah 2002

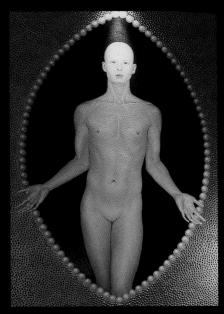

Photographer | Yael Pincus

Situated above the restaurant to which it owes its name—owned by Hassan Abdullah, Michael Lassere and Stefan Karlson—Les Trois Garçons bases its design and decoration on the interests of its three owners in furnishings and artifacts that exemplify the style which has come to be called "new baroque."

The residence is located in a Victorian building in London's Shoreditch. The owners wanted to bring back the glamour of past decades. For designer Hassan Abdullah, it is important to respect the building's soul, to try not to destroy it with an aesthetic that is too contemporary and would depreciate the valuable handmade and historical elements such as the ceiling borders or the original structure. For Abdullah, it is an emotional treasure box. According to the designer, it is important to bring a personal touch to the residence without harming the original atmosphere; therefore, this personal touch has to come from the heart of its creator and not from the latest impersonal aesthetics.

Despite the eclecticism with which the owners have decorated the residence, the ornamentation is heavily influenced, above all, by the French canons of rococo and baroque in spaces such as the living room, the striking bedroom—splashed with ecclesiastic elements—and the bathroom. On the other hand, a small area of the living room, designated for repose and social get-togethers, remains slightly apart, and has been set aside for objects with a more contemporary aesthetic. In this room the colors are more strident and contemporary, pink and red tones coexist alongside pop objects.

1 The living room has been set aside for more informal social gatherings. A more contemporary and familiar decoration allows for relaxation and conversation. The ornamental eclecticism continues.

2|4 In the bathroom, original porcelain pieces have been used for the toilet and washbasin along with modern pieces such as the glass sinks and faucets.

3 Elements and colors from Catholic liturgy, like purple and gold, give the bedroom a provocative atmosphere.

Marianne **Fassler**

Designer | **Marianne Fassler** | Johannesburg, South Africa | 2002

Photographer | Deidi von Schaewen | OMNIA

Marianne Fassler, a well-known South African fashion designer, bases her eclecticism on various African elements, which bring an ethnic touch, and on traditional western decorative components that connect different eras of the twentieth century with contemporary aesthetics.

A special entrance path, flanked on both sides by a wall of braided branches of bomas—knotty trees indigenous to the area—and riverbed stones, foreshadows the atmosphere waiting inside. This property was built in 1920 and is located in a leafy Anglo-Saxon neighborhood of Johannesburg. There is an intense explosion of color in the interior. The living room, painted in a soft yellow tone, goes perfectly with the more intense orange and rosy coloring of the sofa and armchairs. Large, striking pictures by well-known South African artists such as Karel Nel, stand out as does the elaborate fireplace decorated in very lively tones and intertwined branches that add volume while decorating the space. The windows recall the stained-glass windows of a church, converting light into another decorative element.

On the whole the role of the indigenous animal furs and skins is prominent. Examples include the tiger print along the majestic chaise lounge, the zebra print on the armchairs and the omnipresent leopard print on the bedspreads, armchairs, tablecloths, cups and sculptures. The armchairs combine Art Deco shapes and forearms with contemporary upholstery that depicts Jesus Christ alongside African motifs. Other decorative elements such as the coffee table hark back to the 1950s while the bathroom recalls rococo, reaffirming eclecticism in the decorating.

House

1   Two ethnic styles coexist in this house—African and Mexican—Art Deco and kitsch. The house has an extensive collection of African art and contemporary paintings.

2   Most of the details and utensils are not just useful but have an aesthetic quality as well. Many of them are designed by renowned South African artists.

3|4 The mosaic that covers the bathroom wall and the shower floor recalls modernist Catalan art. The mirror, a molded baroque form above the sinks, is an antique.

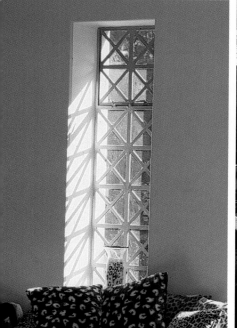

1

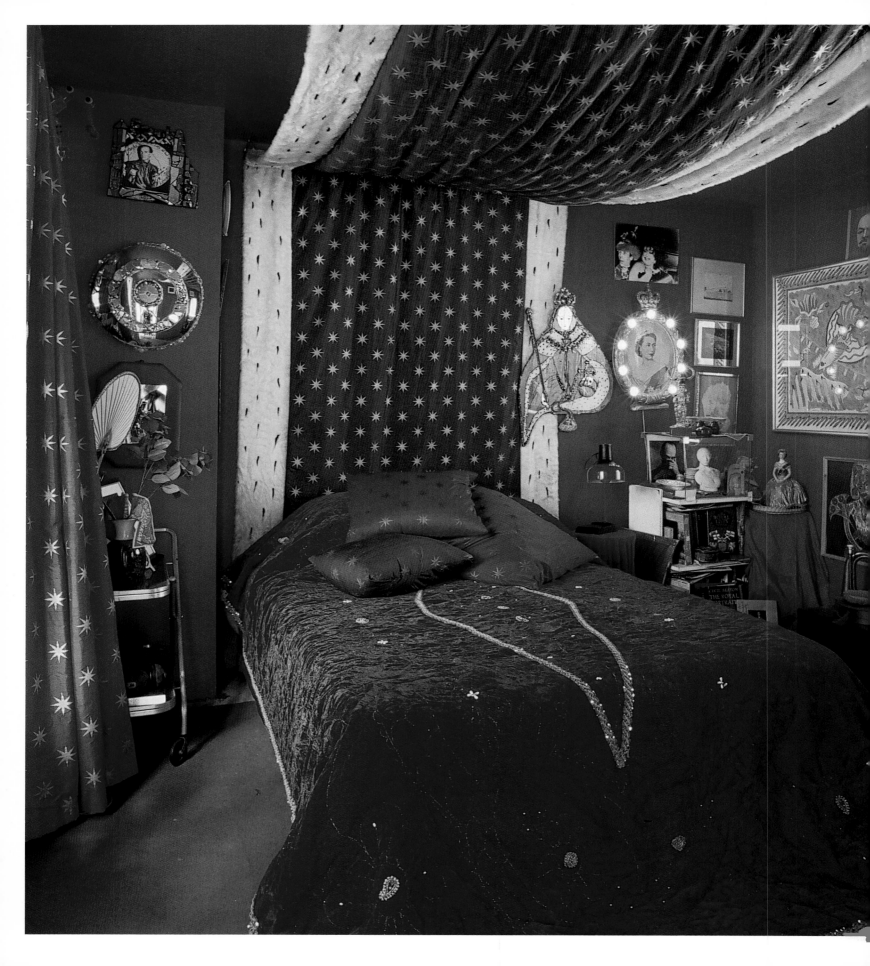

The Glass

Designer | **Michael Davis** | London, UK | 2002

Photographer | Deidi von Schaewen | OMNIA

The house that well-known British sculptor Andrew Logan shares with the designer and ¨urban visionary¨ Michael Davis is located in Bermonsdey, one of the oldest parts of London. When this building was acquired it was a mechanic's workshop, dating back to 1958, and the second floor served as a living space. The final remodeling converted it into a two-story house with two terraces and a glassed-in studio done with aluminum carpentry.

They hung a 1/7-inch-thick glass cover over the second floor ceiling in order to install the sculptor's studio. This elevated the height of the building and balanced it out in relationship to other buildings in the area.

The choice of colors for the walls and the decorative elements are based, in part, on a trip to Mexico: pumpkin, flesh, bright pink, and jade tones bring color and combine with the piece's lighting due to the mirrors and glass which prevail throughout the house. Along the same lines, Andrew Logan's creations are packed with surges of color and light due to the use of mirrors in his sculptures.

The former entrance, kitchen, and dining room have been converted into a series of small rooms with views of the glassed-in studio on the second floor. On the southern façade they put in new windows and arches through which natural light illuminates the interior of the residence, as well as a reinforced concrete staircase up to the studio which is ideal for transporting sculptures as well as for guests´ mobility during social gatherings.

Dwelling

1 In the living room, which is covered by a glass roof, a wide staircase has been installed as well as a small interior balcony which produces the feeling that two levels exist in an ample space.

2 New arches and windows were put in along the southern façade in order to take advantage of the new light source—the glass ceiling—which allows for more luminosity throughout the house.

3 Andrew Logan's sculptures decorate the majority of the rooms where lots of mirrors and glass are used. So, containers and things contained complement one another.

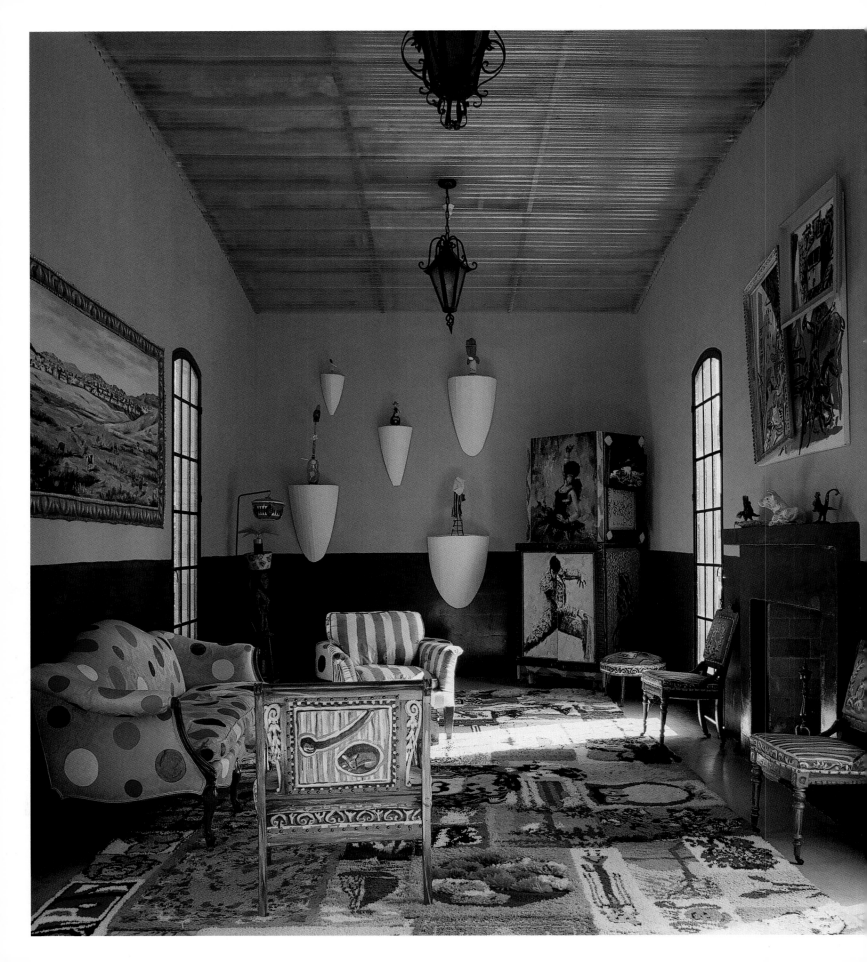

MacConnel-Lowe

Architects | **Ted Smith & Others** | Encinitas, California, USA | 2002

Photographer | Undine Pröhl

The distinguishing feature of the MacConnel-Lowe House is based on the owners' desire to build a residence similar to primitive brick constructions they had seen in the country and in their profession—they are both artists. This symbiosis of austerity in the construction materials as well as in the architectural forms, and the creativity of the inhabitants, characterizes the striking interiors of a home in which the owners' works, bursting with color, have found an exhibition space.

The house, located far back on the lot, is built like a wall that hides a reservoir that is not perceptible until the visitor reaches the house. This creates a surprising effect upon arrival. The yard in front of the house is set aside for cultivation, so the size of the residence had to be reduced and adapted to a narrow, elongated shape. In total, four tall, narrow rooms—10 x 26 feet of surface area and thirteen feet high—based on the type of economic housing this architect has built for years, comprise the conventional environments of a house. The living room and bedroom are located on the extreme ends of the house, east and west respectively. The kitchen is next to the living room, which leads into a vestibule open to the exterior and also connects to the bedroom.

The main bathroom has been placed next to the bedroom, on the east side of the house in a metal tower, which contrasts with the brick used for the rest of the house and, due to its irregular shape, brings an expressionist aspect to the whole.

House

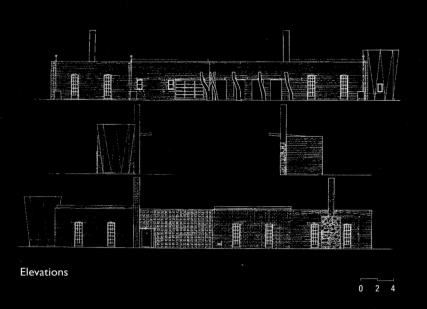

Elevations

0 2 4

2

1 Thanks to the high ceilings and open spaces, the interiors, designed for this house by the owners themselves, are almost identical to installations for museums where these two artists have shown on many occasions.

2|3 The kitchen/dining room, at one end of the house, has many light sources and intensely colored furnishings. The varied red tones in the brick walls provide intensity.

4 In line with using inexpensive but effective materials, the bathroom is a cylinder made of metal sheets that contrast with the brick and create an adjoining ornamental area.

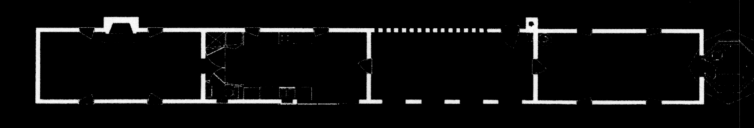

Plan

0 2 4

Oz

Architects | **Grynhaus Architects** | Tel-Aviv, Israel | **2000**

Photographer | Yael Pincus

This apartment, owned by the famous Israeli singer Oz, is located on the third level of an old building in the center of Tel Aviv, in one of the city's typical neighborhoods. The residence reflects the owner's personality, so it combines success, moderate wealth, extreme daringness, and creativity. The basic concept was to create a space in which functionality would complement an atmosphere where the artist would feel motivated creatively. Right in the entrance there are two spaces divided by a long S-shaped wall that separates the living room from the kitchen/dining room. The wall is covered on both sides by paper painted with spectacular landscapes that shake up the senses: seascapes, palm trees, and blue skies in the living room along with yellow tones on the kitchen walls. The floors of these spaces were covered in linoleum in colors that match the rest of the room.

The bedroom and studio are private areas, which remain out of the visitor's view. Each one has been decorated in order to achieve very different atmospheres. On the one hand, the bedroom has been designed with the idea of creating a passionate effect, so red curtains and carpet were used as well as wallpaper painted in black and white with nocturnal and urban landscapes. On the other hand, the studio is done in a sharp green, ideal for igniting creativity and producing an energized psychological state.

The furnishings that decorate the apartment are also done in strong color tones, which empower the space's personality and meet the owner's needs.

Residence

1|2 These two spaces are part of the public areas of the house and correspond with the S-shaped wall that separates the living room from the kitchen/dining room; the former is decorated with tropical landscapes and the latter with forests.

3 An industrial-looking metal curtain separates the living room and the kitchen and combines with the metallic furniture in the second space, where it creates an industrial kitchen aesthetic.

4 The bedroom is one of the house's private spaces. The painted wallpaper recreates the mythic New York skyline and, along with the red curtains, gives the room a feeling of passion.

3

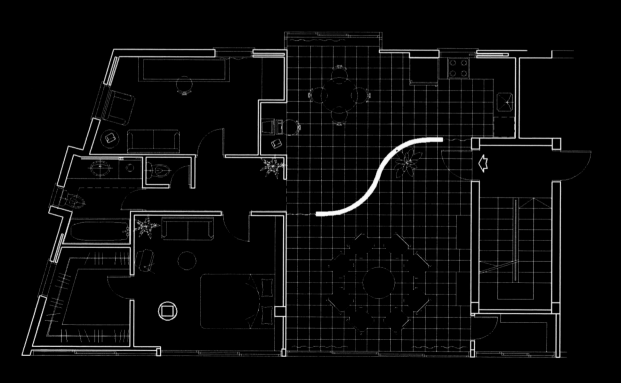

Plan

Staudenmeyer

Designer | **Pierre Staudenmeyer** | Paris, France | 2002

Photographer | Deidi von Schaewen | OMNIA

Located in Paris' tenth arrondissement, very close to the convenient Gare du Nord—which allows the owner frequent trips to New York and London—the design of this apartment is based on the owners collection of objects. The main emphasis falls on each object in and of itself, on each piece chosen by the owner for its uniqueness.

The residence is in an old building from the nineteenth century that helped the architect Georges-Eugène Haussmann give the city one of its many faces and personalities. The mirrors on the doors that separate the rooms of the apartment have been preserved as well as the relief work decorating the walls. The prevailing tone through the whole surface of the house is white, but the intensity of color falls on the ornamental as well as functional objects and accessories.

The decorating scheme mixes pop pieces such as the coffee tables, armchairs, and sofa in the living room, with vases and lamps from seventies funk ambiences. On the floor, the parquet covers almost the entire surface except for a small central area in the living room where the customary rug has been replaced by smooth floor tiles in a pastel blue and light pink pattern. The structure of the house, typical of the first floor in this type of building, provides a large surface area and allows for the combination of ample spaces divided by large doors, which act as dividers but are just walls of glass.

House

1 In the living room, objects from the sixties and seventies—like the British-flag coffee tables—coexist along with vases in classic and popular shapes.

2 The same mix of collector pieces and everyday objects, such as the armchair and futurist footstool alongside decorative dumbbells, exists in all the rooms.

3 The dining room walls are decorated with works of contemporary art; a medium-format photograph next to the fireplace adds a kitschy touch.

House for

Architect | **Brunete Fraccaroli** | São Paulo, Brazil | 2002

Photographer | Tuca Reinés

Despite being very different cities, São Paulo and New York have some things in common, such as the roughness of the environment and a cosmopolitanism created by the need to accommodate people from all over the world. This apartment with a New York essence was designed by Brunete Fraccaroli for a young executive and combines all the features of this architect's work: nerve, light, color, modernity, aestheticism, and investigation in terms of the materials and the possibilities of the space.

One of Fraccaroli's basic design concepts is the recycling of spaces in order to support his design, mainly using furnishings and colored glass that allow for different nuances in the chromatic tones according to the intensity of light or the time of day. The colored glass in this apartment is a dominant feature that helps to create enveloping and seductive atmospheres, and brings a feeling of spaciousness to the space. This designer always undertakes home design from a personal perspective, attending to the needs and requirements of the inhabitant. In this case, he has opted for a versatile structure that separates the living room and bedroom via a panel of green glass within which he has installed a flat, rotating television screen. In this way, the separation of the two environments comes from different points of light, all of which redesign the space on their own. This effect enhances the versatility of the apartment and meets the needs of a young, dynamic, urban woman who is looking for efficiency and convenience in an elegant environment with the luxury that attends her profession.

an Executive

1 Despite having few furnishings, the living room is a great space of expressionist magnitude, due to the daring use of light and colors. The furnishings as well as the ornamental elements are totally contemporary.

2 The photo of a giant eye, which works as a headboard and an ornament, is located directly opposite the rotating flat-screened television that divides the space.

3|4 The kitchen, which is equipped with the most advanced technology, forgoes the use of a lot of objects or traditional ornaments in order to achieve a futurist and austere aesthetic.

3

Ecological **House**

Architect | **Eugene Tsui** | Shenshen, China | 2002

Photographer | Eugene Tsui

The Chinese government commissioned architect Eugene Tsui to design a prototype for a residence that combined ecology and technology with the objective of showing the population the advantages of certain materials used in new construction techniques. Reinforced concrete, polished marble, glass, and smooth river stones were used in the construction of this 219-square-yard volume. From an ecological point of view, there are two fundamental elements: a skylight that allows the resident to control the air currents which ventilate the room, and a pool designed to collect and store rain water. Concurrently, the moist earth also absorbs this water and the residual water, properly treated, is used in the house in the various functions of the bathroom and for watering the indoor plants. The plants, which keep the inside air fresh and clean, are located throughout the entire house and connected by a watering system which constantly recycles water.

The electricity is generated through a series of windmills and photovoltaic panels installed on the roof. The extraordinary illumination comes from the walls through little glass bubbles which shape the streams of light. A stratum of plants creates a natural shade, which softens the intense sunlight from the skylight, and also acts as an acoustic cushion between the rooms. At the same time, translucent glass panels along the upper part of the rooms allow light to enter.

for **the** Future

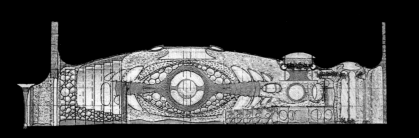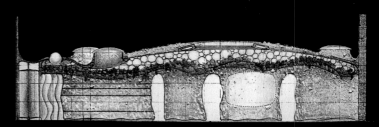

Interior elevations

0 1 2

2

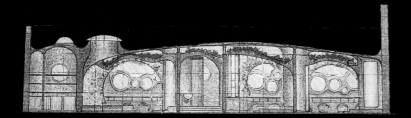

Interior elevations

0 1 2

1   The living room lighting is achieved through many openings in the walls as well as in the ceiling, which allow natural light to pass through, as well as electricity generated by an ecological system installed on the roof.

2   Each atmosphere interacts with the others thanks to the open space design and the uniformity of the light in brown, orange, yellow, and silvery tones that evoke the land formations in this region of China.

3   The open space kitchen is a revolutionary idea in China where cooking has always been done behind closed doors. The objective is to connect this space with the rest of the rooms.

Duggie Fields

Artist | Duggie Fields | London, UK | 2003

Photographer | Deidi von Schaewen | OMNIA

Inhabited by its current owner, British artist Duggie Fields, since 1969, this house is located on a street lined with Edwardian mansions. The residence is made up of three bedrooms, a kitchen, a dining room, a bathroom, and a balcony that contain the interior world of this artist. Fields, the creator of a mini-manifesto about maximalism in art ("MAXIMAlism = minimalism with plus, plus, plus") personalized his house after a trip to New York in 1975. From then on, the colors and figures of his canvasses have taken over different spaces of his house, and the paintings seem to be three-dimensional: the world of painting accesses the real world, the unreal becomes real.

The references and inspirations multiply and draw from a diverse group of sources: Picasso, Dalí, Matisse, Miró, Mondrian, Francis Bacon and Kurt Schwitters, among others. The furnishings, many bought at flea markets, have been refinished and customized, by the artist himself for the most part. The walls are painted white and covered in canvases in many tones, including red, blue, and green, the floor is gray and various paintings accentuate the chromatic contrasts. Fields' arrival at maximalism has been a static journey in time, life in a context that reinvents itself. Lately he has experimented with digital art which has served to enrich this journey.

Residence

1   The door of the living room has been integrated into the decor just like the walls and objects.

2   The customized furnishings and objects are treated in the same way as the walls, creating a three-dimensional effect in the house as a whole.

3   The colorful bathroom reflects a decorating style that never ceases to re-elaborate, producing a symbiosis between work space and living space: the walls are canvases conquered by paint.

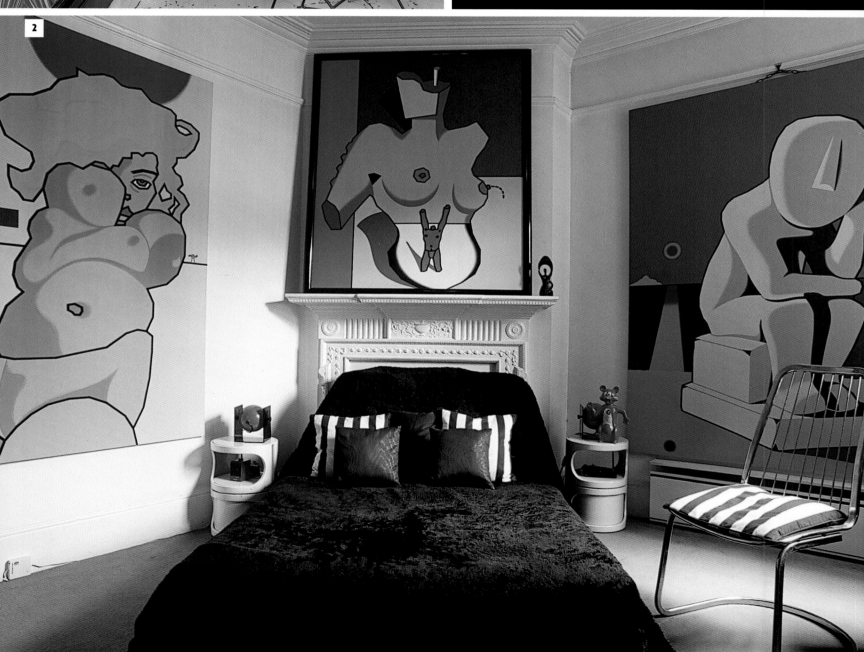

Getter

Designer | **Nimrod Getter** | Tel-Aviv, Israel | 2003

Photographer | Yael Pincus

Intense colors and a focus on fun stand out in this Tel Aviv penthouse decorated by its owner. The intensity of color is especially strong in the kitchen and dining area, which has a long wall painted in strong tones such as yellow, apple green, red, and pink. On the opposite side large windows, which take up almost the entire wall, provide natural light. Shapes and colors identical to those of the wall are painted on the ceiling and the floor is paved in tiles of varying origins, prints, colors, and sizes. Rectangles and squares prevail throughout the space in tiles, windows, and decorative drawings.

In contrast, the work area and living room have been decorated in tones that encourage calm and concentration, like black, white, and the light color of the wood, the only tone used on the walls, ceilings and floors, as well as for the shelves and work table. Furthermore, a strange visual effect has been achieved due to the irregular placement of one of the windows—near the work table—and a large bright red chaise lounge right in the center of the room.

Much of the furniture was made by the owner, like the original kitchen stools, made out of bicycle seats joined by a metal bar, and the curved shelves for kitchen containers.

House

1|2 The windows, divided into rectangles, inspire the straight lines of the wall paintings and the various floor tiles, and create a luminous effect on both the exterior and interior of the house. The owner himself has restored some of the kitchen furniture such as the small tables, shelves, and chairs.

3|4 The living room and a small work area occupy one large space, done in a neutral white tone, where they have installed the computer and library. A long red chaise lounge visually divides the space by facing the living room. Next to the library an irregularly aligned window creates a relaxing optical effect.

1

3

Les **Harris**

Designer and painter | **Les Harris** | Baltimore, Maryland, USA | 2003

Photographer | Jefferson Steele

Charles Leslie Harris´s studio museum is a clear example of chromatic maximalism in its purest form of expression. The whole space is taken up by the installation, "The Labyrinth of Amaranthine." A painter, Harris is a 79-year-old retired art professor in Baltimore who has been working on the yet-to-be-finished piece for twenty-six years straight—a compendium of his creative philosophy.

The labyrinth consists of sixteen rooms in an old Baltimore factory, all of which are decorated with works of art. The images recreate details or even entire scenes from ancient Egypt, the Chartres Cathedral and the Notre Dame, the Sistine Chapel, the Uffizi Palace, and the Roman Coliseum . . . a journey through art history.

During a visit to the Chartres Cathedral in France, the force of the light projected through the cathedral's beautiful windows confounded Harris. From that moment on he has dedicated his life and work to the constant, obsessive search for the re-creation of those colors in his work and space, along with a very personal mystic development influenced by Christian Science and quantum physics.

The paintings found in "The Labyrinth of Amaranthine" are not limited to conventional locations such as canvases, walls, or wood. They are all over—on furniture, columns, folding screens, chairs—and inundate the entire space like a chromatic flood.

Studio

1   Seeing the rose window at the Chartres Cathedral was the genesis of Les Harris´s investigation into color. The objects´ symbology express the artist's reality.

2   This room, called "The Age of the Novel," is decorated with large, striking paintings done on top of much smaller frames in a collage-like form.

3   The objective of the "Labyrinth of Amaranthine" is to materialize the maxim of quantum physics that proclaims that reality is not local. The columns illustrate ancient history.

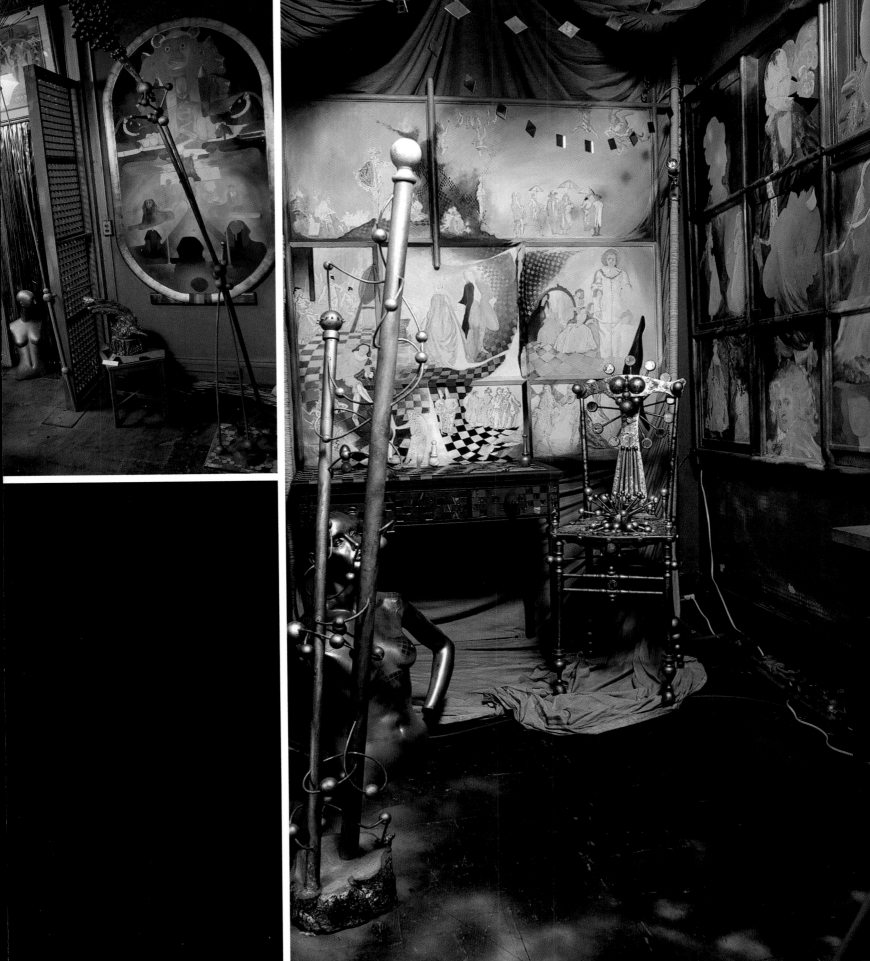

Amauri Jr.

Architect | **Brunete Fraccaroli** | São Paulo, Brazil | 2001

Photographer | Tuca Reinés

Brunete Fraccaroli's main objective when designing the interior of this residence was to create contexts that could be lived in and not just to develop an impractical, aesthetic space. Therefore in this house, owned by a well-known São Paulo television personality, everything is distributed and decorated with a focus on relaxation in order to counteract long, tiring days of social and business events.

As a complement to this facet, there are also areas for social activities, like the ample living room with large sofas, which allow people to have relaxed conversations. In this space the strength of the decorating rests on the furnishings, accessories, and decorative elements; thanks to those elements, any change in the decorating is economically feasible and done from the purely functional side of things. However, Fraccaroli avoided ornamental elements, in regard to the objects as well as the walls.

In order to differentiate the private and common spaces the designer used different decorating styles. The private area, used for watching movies or television programs in general, is bolder and more playful in its design: the flat-screen television has been installed over the fireplace (the use of modern equipment allows us to conquer new architectonic spaces), the walls are painted strident colors and the design of the armchairs helps to create a space focused on fun. In contrast, the large salon, set aside for social gatherings, is predominantly white, creating a space for rest and relaxation, and the simplicity of the furnishings allows it to be an open ambience.

House

1 An ample space allows for the contrast between the sparse furnishings and their large size.

2 The use of glass in the decorating scheme helps generate a relaxing atmosphere in the area set aside for social affairs.

3 An equilibrium in the decor is achieved using polar opposites: dark and light, hot and cold, volume and emptiness; these contrasts allow for a dynamic design.

1

Stencil

Photographer | Deidi von Schaewen | OMNIA

This house holds one of the most extensive collections of artistic stencils in Europe—"the most democratic art form," according to Helen Morris. The owners wanted to fit a wide array of examples of this technique in the house, which constitutes an interesting journey through the art of stenciling and is a reflection of the personality of each of the owners. So Rachel Morris' rooms are coquettish atmospheres in pastel tones; Michael Chippendale creates a pacific, tidy opulence; and Helen Morris decorates with bright colors.

The room decorated in a Chinese motif was inspired by the interior paintings in the royal pavilion of Brighton Palace, which dates back to the eighteenth century. The Indian and Ottoman rooms evoke England in 1960; in the former intentionally empty frames that once held photographs of the Beatles recall a mythic past. The latter has been decorated with stencils from floor to ceiling using a water-based paint protected by several layers of varnish as well as velvet, silk, and gold and copper colored paint which results in a crafty, exuberant room.

The dining room has been decorated with stencils that bring back the British nineteenth century and pay homage to artists of that era including William Morris and Walter Crane, whose portraits hang on the walls of this room along with those of some of their contemporaries.

A theatrical effect was sought out through the entire house; one of the places where it was best achieved is in the bathroom pertaining to Rachel Morris' area, where she has used pearl-toned paint along with chandeliers and gleaming silks.

Residence

1 Designed by Michael Chippendale, the Raj room recreates the exoticism of India with carved wooden elephant chairs and velvet cushions. The walls reproduce Hindu decorating motifs.

2 The Arabian Nights bedroom, similar to a Hollywood set, is covered in silk and velvet with gold prints. The floor is also decorated with stencils.

3 Continuing with a decorating style that alludes to faraway places and an adventurous spirit, a large navigation map covers one of the bathroom walls.

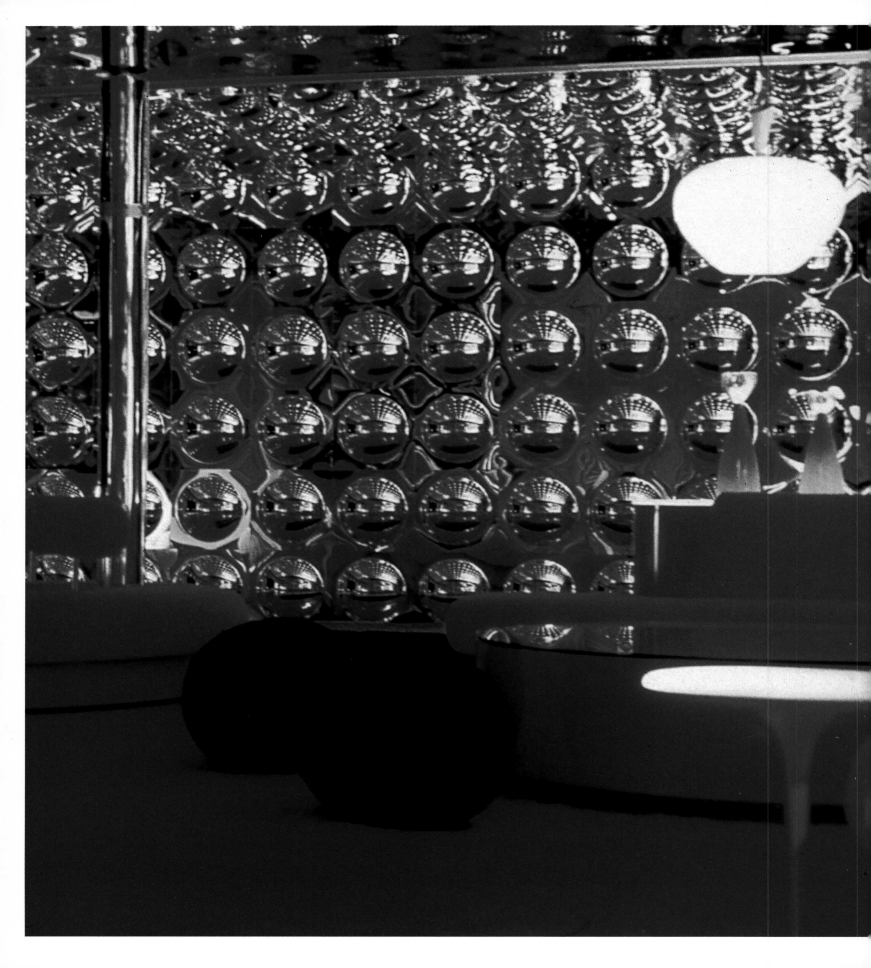

Lenny **Kravitz**

Architects | **Michael Czysz, Architropolis** | Miami, Florida, USA | 1999

Photographer | Architropolis

Michael Czysz, the architect and designer whom some have baptized the "master of maximalism," based musician Lenny Kravitz's Miami home on the concepts of sensuality, seduction, and play. For Czysz, an interior is an environment or atmosphere that shelters the person who inhabits it; therefore, this retro-futurist house is designed with an aesthetic that is very similar to the owner's. The forms of the furniture, due to their volume and color, recall a seventies aesthetic. It all brings a funky and sensual style to the house, and this is what was lacking from Czysz's roots: minimalism and an admiration for the Bauhaus school.

The objective of the architect, an admirer of Philippe Starck, was to create an environment that would have an emotional impact for visitors passing through this house. Therefore, he used materials that could be categorized as strange or extravagant. None of the materials, of which there is a huge variety, received special attention: from stainless steel to suggestive fabrics, from plastics to special cloths. The surroundings create an exciting atmosphere, while the humid climate and the views along with the constant presence of music complement the quest for sensuality.

Czysz likes taking risks—we could say it is what makes him tick creatively—and he likes to get into his clients' interior world in order to reproduce it in their spaces. Usually Czysz creates ninety percent of the furnishings decorating his houses; this time he even designed a silver guitar that goes with the style of the residence.

House

1 Artificiality was also chosen for the pool, the silvery color of the metallic sheets reflects on the water and vice versa, creating a reflecting visual trick.

2 The bedroom is closed off from natural light; the walls are completely covered in tiny mirrors that reflect the set of lights installed in this space.

Plan

0   2   4

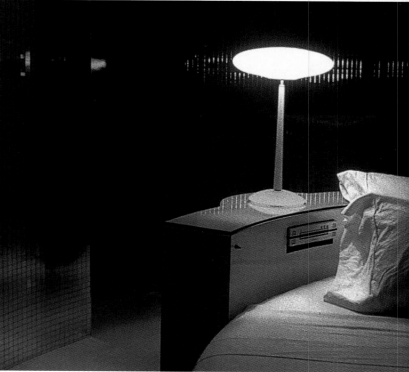

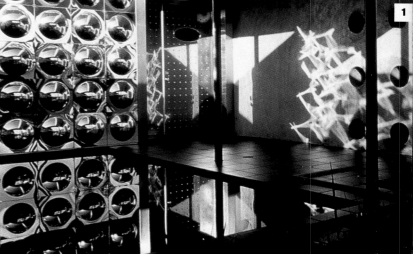

2

Collinance

Designer | **Pierre Peyrolle** | Collinance, France | 2002

Photographer | Deidi von Schaewen | OMNIA

In the restoration of the Collinance Castle, an extraordinary piece from France's grand siecle (the seventeenth and eighteenth centuries), Pierre Peyrolle took a phrase that architect Vittorio Mazzucconi used to define his own work as doctrine: "A discourse about the memory of architecture." He pays special homage to the work of Mazzucconi and, at the same time, finds a place to openly salute his aesthetic exhibitionism. The architect's objective was to endow the castle with a baroque context capable of evoking the memory of an era, and while he was at it, revise the concept of contemporary architecture.

He maintained the austerity of the façade in order to preserve the magnificence that the castle keeps behind its walls, visible only to those invited to pass through the doors. The vegetation that extends throughout the surrounding, a 44-acre forest, acts as an exuberant wall of protection.

The influence of the German classical composer Wagner is an important element in the decorating scheme: the strength and passion of his music shape the disproportion of many of the ornamental elements. Insane and visceral are two other adjectives which connect Wagner to the decor in some of the rooms of the castle, such as the sumptuous salon, in which the voluptuous black and silver chairs, with inlay work in purple and lapis lazuli inspired by Florence museum pieces, along with a multitude of mirrors that amplify the space, help to create this theatrical, exaggerated effect.

Castle

1. The staircase, which starts in a room decorated with German renaissance drawings, was created in white and gold tones. It maintains the designs and connects the piece to a scarlet study.

2. The Louis XIII-style salon is done in black marble and mirrors, fake crimson malachite and lapis lazuli; the table is done in marble in-laid work. In total, twenty-seven yards of exuberance.

3. The images used in the decor carry a heavy symbolist, religious, and sometimes Masonic weight. A large angel keeps vigil over the person sleeping in this bed.

3

Dwelling in

Architect | **Brian Housden** | London, UK | 1965-2003

Photographers | Dennis Gilbert / VIEW,
Brian Housden

This house is located in Hampstead, a London neighborhood filled with Victorian constructions and some of the first modernist houses from 1930. The area was bombed heavily during World War II. The residence was built separately from the rest of the buildings due to the instability of its foundation. The exterior structure was built between 1963 and 1965, but the decoration and some interior renovations continue as works-in-progress.

Because of the foundation problems, concrete was used to build the house. This material, which up until then had only been used to construct office buildings or skyscrapers, allowed for the creation of large spaces in the interior. Heavy, brightly colored curtains hanging from metal rods, similar to those used in hospital rooms, separate the spaces where privacy is needed, such as the living and dining rooms. One of the most striking elements is the natural lighting system. The designers tried to make the best use of the light by using constructive technologies, which actually diminish the spectacular views from the interior. As a result, the views are filtered through semi-opaque Nevada glass walls and narrow Critall metal windows, which allow for seductive and fragmented glimpses of the exterior.

A mix of elements from various sources were used in the decorating, such as fifties furniture by Dutch designer Gerrit Rietveld, the white glass mosaic, semi-opaque glass lenses, shredded metal windowpanes, and the exposed electric system and pipes. The house is also filled with symbolic elements that decorate the space, for example, Mandala circles carved out of the concrete floor in the dining area within the living room and around the bed in the master bedroom.

South Hill Park

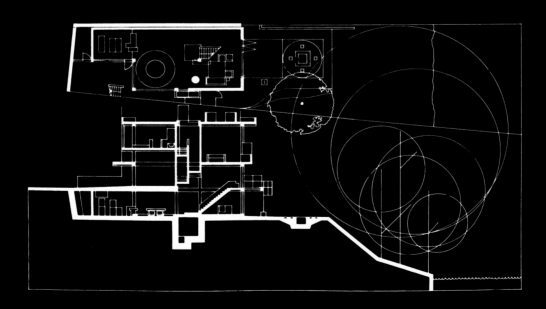

Basement and section

0 2 4

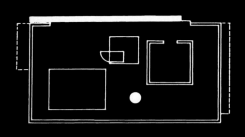

Second floor

First floor

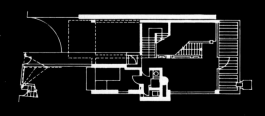

Ground floor

0 1 2

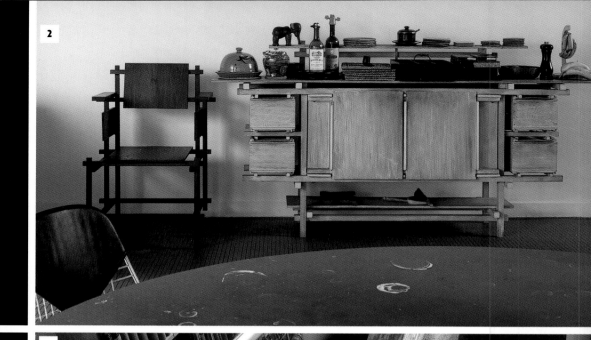

4

1   The water and heating pipes are exposed in order to enhance the feeling of an industrial space that the exposed concrete creates.

2   The top of the dining room table was created with two identical semi-circular pieces of polished Irish slate with an inlay of oyster and fern fossils.

3|4   The concrete mold of the staircase wall is decorated with white, green, yellow, pink, and black Norwegian marble.

Estevão

Designer | **Estevão** | São Paulo, Brazil | 2003

Photographer | Tuca Reinés

São Paulo, like any modern metropolis, houses two worlds: the rich one that advances technologically by leaps and bounds, and the world of the poor who live in the shadow of progress. This is the case of Paraisoplois, an enclave of shacks in the wealthy neighborhood of Morumbi in the largest city in Brazil. Estevão House is the product of fifteen years of work on the part of the owner who is from Bahía and works as a piping installer. Aside from this, Estevão is also an intuitive, self-taught architect who has built his house with few resources and a lot of imagination. Judging from certain parts of the house, one would think Estevão was an admirer of Gaudí, however he had never seen the work of this other visionary.

The materials used to construct the house are mostly recycled and come from nature, such as the tree trunks, which are decorated with stones and paintings and form the arched columns of a path that connects the entranceway to the central piece; and the sculptures made with stones and other ornamental elements that contribute to the feeling of majesty and fantasy.

The star shape rules among all the shapes and colors, on the ceilings as well the walls. Star shapes also decorate the doors of the house, and other furnishings such as chairs and tables.

House

1. Estevão has created an ornamentation that often imitates natural motifs; like this room where the vegetation and its colors blur with the natural tones.

2. At the entrance, two recycled statues welcome visitors. The baroque qualities of the forms blur with the exuberance of the vegetation.

3. The same natural resources are inside and out: drawn from materials such as pebbles and wood, now painted and colorful.

1

Teresa Sepulcre

Designer | **Teresa Sepulcre** | Elche, Spain | 2003

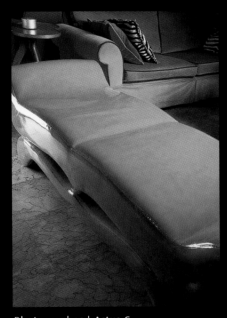

Photographer | Artur G

Teresa Sepulcre, a furniture and accessory designer, has taken big risks with this house, which is bathed in the spirit and colors of the Mediterranean, by giving precedence to artificial light over natural light.

The decorative concept consists of creating the ambience of a nightclub within the residence. As a result, the ornamental resources are centered, almost exclusively, around the furnishings—also designed by Teresa Sepulcre—which vary from bright yellow to intense red, and blue. In order to achieve this nightclub atmosphere, the furniture was given a starring role, and it stands out due to its curved shapes and strong colors, to the detriment of other ornamental elements such as vases, pictures, and figurines. Wall lamps are used to imitate the lighting characteristic of such atmospheres. They supply an indirect projection of light and envelop the surroundings.

The absence of details is intentional, since the objective is to achieve a nightclub setting where decoration is usually provided by colors and furnishings. This idea extends to the kitchen and bathroom as well, where we find the same absence of detail from which the chromatic exuberance benefits.

The use of color extends to the walls, where intense blues and yellows provide the whole with exuberance in order to solidify one of the maxims of the designer: "Long live the new baroque!"

House

1|2 Two cupboards designed by Teresa Sepulcre: the first, due to its shape, is called Croche, and the second, divided into two parts, Crazy Heart.

3 Plastic is the material that has been used most in the decorating of this house, including for the wardrobe in this room. Accessories and decorative elements have been left out in order to focus on the ornamental force of the furniture.

1

2

Edelman

Designers | **M. Bonetti, E. Garouste** | Architect | **J. Richter** | Leman Lake, Switzerland | 2002

Photographer | Deidi von Schaewen | OMNIA

This house belongs to Asher Edelman, a New York businessman and contemporary art collector, and his wife, Regina. It is an old dry cleaner's from the beginning of the twentieth century that was originally composed of two main parts and now, after a restoration by architect Jacques Richter, has 1,640 square yards of exhibition space in addition to the rooms of the common residence.

Eclecticism and a combination of different elements from different eras characterize the decoration of this house, where aesthetically different objects and furnishings from various origins coexist: for example, the large, circa 1930s table in the central room near the entrance, along with contemporary objects by Mattia Bonetti and Elisabeth Garouste, such as the table and armchairs covered in colt skin—part of the Rodeo series for Neotu—as well as a colt skin rug.

In the living room, an enormous rug of pure virgin wool and various sofas and armchairs from the Patchwork collection by these designers for the B.G.H. edition provide the atmosphere with warmth and color. Over the fireplace hangs a painting by French painter Jean Dubuffet and on the opposite wall one by a Catalan, Miquel Barceló.

The first floor walls have been covered in raffia in order to preserve their natural tone and the aged parquet has been varnished ebony.

They have paid close attention to everyday household items such as the tea and coffee set, designed by Richard Meyer, the fabric of the placemats by artist Willem de Kooning, and the 1930s silverware from Tiffany & Co.

Dwelling

1 Garouste e Bonetti designed Fall Leaves, the large virgin wool rug in the living room, as well as the Patchwork Collection divan for the B.G.H. Edition.

2 The house holds the museum of The Asher Edelman Foundation, which aims not only to provide space for pieces from the private collection, but to provide an exhibition space for contemporary artists as well.

3 The central room, next to the entrance, includes a large 1930s Italian designer table that Regina Edelman found in New York. A Joseph Beuys´ work, dated 1963, hangs on the left-hand wall.

1

Virgina **Bates**

Designer | **Virginia Bates** | London, UK | 2003

Photographer | Deidi von Schaewen | OMNIA

The decadence and sophistication of the decor in this house takes us back to nineteenth-century London. The house is situated in a Victorian-era building that preserves the architectural and ornamental elements such as the relief work on the walls and ceilings. The excess in the details and decorating makes this residence a magnificent example of maximalism in ornamental details. The use of color is more abundant in the library where the walls, ceilings and some of the furniture, like the voluptuous sofa, are purple-toned while in the rest of the house pastel tones prevail, overall light pink and various ranges of beige.

There are some noteworthy finishes on some of the ceilings, for example in the bathroom and library where tapestries have been used to cover the whole surface and contribute to creating a feeling of saturation and decorative excess. In general, the tapestries and fabrics are decorative elements that bring exuberance and voluptuousness to the whole.

The designers have maintained the original elements including the floor patterns, hallways, and bathrooms, and furniture such as wardrobes and tables. In this house, the most significant element in the architecture and decoration is the timelessness, the disconnection from the era in which it actually exists. Everything here represents a journey into the past, a way of understanding reality and a yearning for an age that was more splendid, more elegant, than our own.

Residence

1 The bathroom shows the emphasis on detail, richness, prosperity, power of seduction, and the refinement of the decadent style of the late nineteenth century.

2 The bedroom responds to Paul Verlaine's definition of decadence: 'Everything shines in purple and gold.' The bedroom furniture and decorative objects evoke voluptuousness and wealth.

3 The living room exemplifies the extreme style that made size and contours the expressive form of an age that eventually came grinding to a halt.

Marie **Beltrami**

Designer | **Marie Beltrami** | Paris, France | 2002

Photographer | Deidi von Schaewen

The house is located in a two-hundred-year-old building in Paris, whose walls once held a brothel. The paintings on the walls, which simulate frescoes from Roman antiquity, were found eighteen years ago when the wallpaper that had covered them for years was removed. The owner decided to preserve them because they carried an important artistic value and gave the residence personality, so they covered the frescoes in gold patina stain that protects against the wear of time.

Two decorative, snake-shaped, wall lamps acquired in Marrakesh are installed at either end of the bed and provide the bedroom with subdued lighting. Following her own instinctual decorating style, the owner painted a human figure in black on one of the walls. The crown hanging over the bed comes from an ancient theater. The majority of the furniture and decorative objects have been acquired in secondhand markets, the metal night tables, for example, came from a convent. In order to enhance the decor, which was inspired by the past, the designer has chosen silk in beige tones that heighten the room's subtle opulence.

The Roman wall fresco, framed between vermilion tulle and nylon curtains, dominates the red room. The floor in this room is covered in mahogany wax. The crack in the fresco located above the fireplace has simply been painted yellow, following the owner's creative instinct.

House

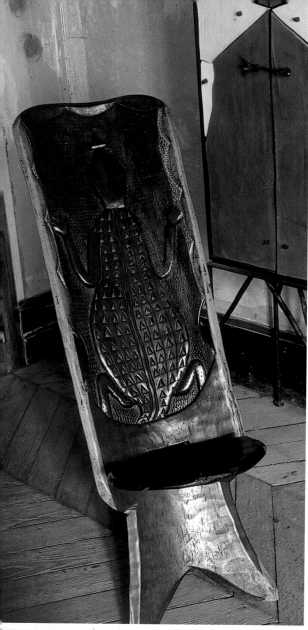

1. The frescoes, which recreate paintings from Pompeii, and date from the eighteenth century, have been preserved by the patina that has developed over time, without any sort of restoration.

2. The designers applied a coat of gilded wax to the bedroom wall and kept the base that remained after eliminating the painted paper that was there when the apartment was acquired.

3. The small bed that has been placed in a corner of the apartment is an original piece from the Napoleonic era. Military officials used to rest in it.

Somoroff

Architect | **S. Alastair Wanta** | Collaborator | **J. Ellinger** | New York City, USA | 2000

Photographer | Klaus Frahm/ARTUR

The owner of this Soho loft is a photographer and filmmaker with a special interest in Jewish mysticism and quantum physics, upon which the basic design concepts of this project are based. The loft is situated within the parameters of sculptural architecture, in which mass and geometric shapes provide the space with ornamentation. The graded or serrated form of the masses is due to explanations offered by the cabala about the process of creation. The lighting has been designed so that each segment of light is associated with the idea of emanation combined with the different construction materials such as wood, metal, and glass.

Keeping to the theories of the cabala, the walls, ceiling, and floor have been imagined as a three-dimensional photograph. Against this saturation of volume the choice of furniture balances out the decor and the architecture; due to this the furniture is designed with straight, clear lines that let the space breathe.

The whole residence is structured around the dining room, a central place in Jewish homes for traditional celebrations. The living room, study, kitchen, bedrooms, and playroom surround this central spot.

Loft

1   The distribution of mass used in the design process was
    determined by various paths between the different volumes;
    this emphasizes location, width, and length.

2   In the kitchen, equipped for traditional Jewish rituals, painted plaster
    prevails along with other materials like wood, metal, and glass.

3   The living room and kitchen share an open space where the
    partitioning lines of the structure define the different areas.

Pompeii

Designer | **Christopher Drew** | Bristol, UK | 2003

Photographer | Julie Phipps/VIEW

This Bristol apartment illustrates in the present, some moments from Britain's past: a fascination with the classical world, especially Venice and Italy, awoke in England starting in the eighteenth century. The wall frescoes reproduce first century B.C. classical paintings from Pompeii, as do some ornamental elements like sculptures and vessels.

The house completely recreates and mixes various chronological periods during which classical references, full of elegance and nobility, marked British aesthetic canons. We also find examples of decorating from the nineteenth century, such as photographs in antique frames and ornamental relief work.

Earth and ochre tones prevail along with some green representing Pompeiian paintings in the wall frescoes in the hallway and other interiors. This use of color brings realism, along with a subtle theatricality, and magnificence to the whole. In the rooms with wall frescoes, decoration has been kept to a minimum in order to highlight the paintings.

The bathroom is decorated with a timelessness that is reflected in each and every detail; there are candlesticks on the bathtub and painted red paper on the walls evoking the inside cover of an ancient book.

The large drapes reiterate this determination to excavate a world and age lost forever. The use of different sculptures and ornamental reliefs recapture a classical style that no longer exists beyond these walls and makes this apartment into an aesthetic refuge.

Apartment

1   Theatricality is a very relevant factor in this apartment, where the use of curtains reinforces the idea of representation while evoking an air of mystery.

2   A reproduction of the ¨Venus de Milo¨ statue, from classical Greece, illustrates the spiritual journey toward Latin and Greek antiquity that this ornamentation proposes.

3   The black marble contrasts against the intense red of the painted paper, which recalls the inside covers of books published in the eighteenth and nineteenth centuries.